MW00324035

Grandma's Storybook

Wisdom, Wit, and Words of Advice

Plain Sight Publishing
an Imprint of Cedar Fort, Inc.
Springville, Utah

ISBN 13: 978-1-4621-1800-7

Published by Plain Sight Publishing, an imprint of Cedar Fort, Inc., 2373 W. 700 S., Springville, UT 84663
Distributed by Cedar Fort, Inc., www.cedarfort.com

LIBRARY OF CONGRESS CONTROL NUMBER: 2015954717

Cover design by Lauren Error
Page design by Krystal Wares
Cover design © 2016 by Cedar Fort, Inc.
Edited by Eileen Leavitt

Printed in the U.S.A.

10 9 8 7 6 5 4 3 2 1

Printed on acid-free paper

To: _____

From: _____

Contents

Introduction

Imagine that you know you are going to pass away tomorrow, and you have today, and only today, to document your entire life story. You will be allowed to fill a carry-on suitcase with everything you can fit into it that you want to pass on to future generations of your family. This might be the only record they will have of who you were, what you did for a living, who you loved, or what your values were. Your great-grandchildren will know you only based on what you condense into this one small space. What would you put in it?

Just for fun, try it. Get a small suitcase and set a timer for twenty minutes. Gather your most prized possessions and family heirlooms. Put in your favorite photo albums, the video that documents the birth of your first child, the plate with the footprints of your first grandchild, and the silver watch handed down from your grandfather. Dig through your file cabinet and pull out your college diploma and your marriage certificate. Rummage through boxes in the basement or attic until you find your college letterman's sweater, the carved bowl you purchased on your honeymoon, and the treasured doll you got for Christmas when you were five.

What about the stack of Christmas cards you saved from the first year you were away at college, the sheaf of letters and postcards your husband mailed to you while you were dating, or the copy of your master's thesis? Once you are finished, stand back and smile. You've gathered all the things you own that are most important to you. But here's the problem. Even this treasury of important items is not likely to have meaning to anyone else, because something important is still missing: the stories.

• The watch your parents gave you as a graduation gift has long since stopped working. Your kids might throw it away if you don't let them know your dad went without lunch for six months to save the money to buy it.

• The photo of you at Yellowstone National Park preserves an image of what you looked like, but does it tell the story about how you hitchhiked to get there?

• The ticket stub from a double feature at the Egyptian Theatre is meaningless to anyone who doesn't understand that you saved it because it was the first date you had with your husband.

The memories that are important to you will only be important to the people you love if you share the stories that give them meaning. That is what this book is for. Between the pages of this book, you'll record some of those precious stories and compile, day by day, a history of some of your most important moments.

"This might be the only record they will have of who you were, what you did for a living, who you loved, or what your values were."

With over three hundred question prompts, plus pages designed to help you involve your children and grandchildren in the story-gathering process, the memories you record here are destined to become someone else's most prized possession. Enjoy the journey you are about to take—a journey to record and remember your life's most important moments. Fill out just one page per day, or pick and choose topics that are interesting to you and fill them out in any order. Scribble out the original question prompt and write in one of your own if you like. This is your history, after all.

As you write, you'll be reminded of other stories you want to record, and there may or may not be a question prompt in the book that will help you remember that story. To make sure these treasured stories are not forgotten, use the "That Reminds Me" sheets, starting on page 181, to jot down your own story prompts so you can remember to include those stories too.

This book is organized by topic rather than by date, and that's by design. Of course your children will want to know what day you were born and who your parents were. That's why most personal histories start that way. But we prefer to let you dive right in and start recounting memories we know your grandchildren will love. Rather than being a book that records just names and dates, this book is designed to record stories— your stories.

To give everyone in the family a little extra incentive to make sure this book doesn't get tucked away empty to gather dust, we've also included some family-friendly activities that will get the entire family involved in the story-gathering process. Some of these activities use technologies like mobile applications. Don't worry if you aren't comfortable with the technology. Your grandchildren probably are. The point is to have some fun family time as you work together to create your living history.

NOTE: If you are giving a copy of this book to your grandmother as a gift, please see the activity "The Most Important Thing about Grandma" on page 55. You may choose to give members of your family an opportunity to write their own thoughts in this section prior to gifting the book to your grandma.

Family Stories

Describe your most memorable family vacation.

What was your most disastrous family vacation? Do you remember a vacation mishap you can laugh about today?

Which sibling were you closest to?

_____

_____

_____

Describe your parents' work. What did your mother
do? What did your father do for a living?

_____

_____

_____

_____

_____

_____

_____

_____

_____

_____

What do you remember most about watching your
father work around the house or in the yard?

_____

_____

_____

_____

_____

_____

_____

_____

_____

_____

What one-on-one experience with your mother stands out
in your memory?

_____

_____

_____

_____

_____

_____

_____

_____

_____

_____

_____

_____

_____

_____

What were some family expectations growing up?

_____

_____

_____

_____

_____

_____

_____

_____

_____

Were you named after anyone? What does your name mean?

_____

_____

_____

_____

_____

Do you have a nickname? If so, who gave it to you?

_____

_____

_____

_____

What was your favorite family car?

_____

_____

_____

What do you remember about the day a loved one died?
What was the first family funeral you ever attended?

_____

_____

_____

_____

_____

_____

_____

_____

_____

_____

_____

_____

_____

_____

Write down one thing you would specifically leave to each of your children, as if you had no last will and testament.

_____

_____

_____

_____

_____

_____

_____

_____

_____

_____

_____

What children's book did your kids ask you to read again and again to them?

_____

_____

_____

<u>What are your children's names? How did you decide</u>
<u>on each of their names?</u>

Family Traditions

What are some of your favorite Christmas traditions in your family?

When did you stop believing in Santa Claus?

How did Santa leave your gifts? Were they wrapped? Labeled?

_____

_____

_____

_____

_____

_____

_____

_____

Next to Christmas or Hanukkah, what was your favorite holiday?

_____

_____

_____

_____

_____

_____

How did you most often celebrate the Fourth of July?

_____

_____

_____

Write down any quirky traditions your family keeps when family members have a birthday.

What was your most memorable costume for Halloween?

How much money would the tooth fairy leave under your pillow? What would you buy with it?

_____

_____

_____

_____

What New Year's Eve do you remember the most? Why was it so memorable?

_____

_____

_____

_____

_____

_____

_____

What Thanksgiving tradition did you carry on with your own family?

_____

_____

_____

_____

What is your favorite kind of pie on Thanksgiving?

What was your favorite holiday to celebrate as a family?

Did you pray together as a family? How did that change your relationship with your parents and siblings?

_____

_____

_____

_____

_____

_____

_____

_____

_____

_____

_____

Did you attend church each week?

_____

_____

_____

_____

_____

_____

Can you recall any other family traditions that were unique to your family?

_____

_____

_____

_____

_____

_____

_____

_____

_____

_____

_____

_____

_____

_____

_____

_____

_____

_____

_____

Activity
The Grandma Treasure Hunt

A Hunt to Help Your Grandchildren Discover
the Whereabouts of Your Most Prized Possessions

Make a treasure map or create a treasure hunt (complete with clues) for your grandchildren to participate in the next time they visit your home. Before you start, consider what items are in your home that you would consider treasures—perhaps treasures no one else knows about. You may need to dig through your attic or sock drawer to find things that even you have forgotten about. If you are comfortable with the idea, allow your grandchildren to rummage about your house. Have them bring items to you that they find interesting. Consider labeling some of these items to let grandchildren know who you would like to inherit them in the future.

This is not necessarily a treasure hunt to find things that will have value to other people. This is a treasure hunt to document things that are valuable to YOU and the reasons why. Something as simple as a beautiful cup and saucer or an old pair of your eyeglasses could become a treasure to your grandchildren. Once you are gone, even a single tangible item that once belonged to you will give them a connection to you and a story to tell their own grandchildren. Remember, all it really takes to turn something into an heirloom is a story and time.

Do you have any of the following items in your home just waiting to become an heirloom?

☐ paintings and other works of art

☐ silver, china, or crystal

☐ jewelry and other personal items that are important to you, regardless of their cash value

☐ photographs and photo albums

☐ valuable books (early and first-edition copies, signed copies, or just your favorites)

☐ family Bible

☐ medals and trophies

☐ photos of the first car you owned

☐ gowns, coats, uniforms, or articles of clothing you have saved

- [ ] favorite music or albums

- [ ] glasses, watches, or things that stopped working but you kept anyway

- [ ] old slides, DVDs, VHS tapes, cassette tapes, or computer disks you have saved because of their historical significance

- [ ] gifts you received for your wedding

- [ ] items given to you by a special friend or acquaintance

- [ ] something your husband gave you as a gift while you were courting or as an anniversary gift

- [ ] vintage toys or games you have saved

- [ ] anything handed down to you by your own parents or grandparents

Childhood & Elementary School

Where were you born?

What was unique about your birth?

What is your earliest memory?

What was the name of the elementary school you attended?

_____

_____

Who was your favorite elementary school teacher? What was especially memorable about that teacher, and what did you appreciate most about him or her?

_____

_____

_____

_____

_____

_____

_____

_____

_____

_____

_____

_____

Did you earn any awards or recognitions when you were in elementary school (prior to age twelve)?

How did you prefer to spend your time at recess?

Is there a memorable school or church performance you participated in as a child?

Who was your best friend in elementary school? What fun things do you remember doing with that friend?

_____

_____

_____

_____

_____

_____

_____

What was a common after-school activity you participated in?

_____

_____

_____

_____

_____

_____

_____

_____

_____

How long did it take you to get to and from school? How did you get there? Do you have a memorable experience related to getting back and forth from school?

_____

_____

_____

_____

_____

_____

_____

What stands out in your memory about the playground, principal, or anything else about the school?

_____

_____

_____

_____

_____

_____

Describe your school lunch. What was in it? Who made it?

How did you celebrate Halloween, Valentine's Day, or other holidays at school?

Did you have any pets? What were their names? Describe a happy or sad event with one of them.

What did you want to be when you grew up?

Did you play a musical instrument as a child?

What is the worst thing you ever did that you never got in trouble for because no one but you knew about it?

_____

_____

_____

_____

_____

_____

_____

What is something you hesitated telling your parents about for fear of being punished? Did you confess later?

_____

_____

_____

_____

_____

_____

_____

_____

_____

What was your favorite thing to wear as a child?

_____

_____

_____

Do you have a birthday that stands out as particularly memorable? Why?

_____

_____

_____

_____

_____

_____

Describe a time when you went with a parent to buy groceries.

_____

_____

_____

_____

_____

How much did a postage stamp cost when you were a child?

_____

_____

Who cut your hair when you were growing up?
What was your most embarrassing hairstyle
as a child?

_____

_____

_____

_____

_____

Describe a typical day at
kindergarten.

_____

_____

_____

_____

What did you do during school holidays?

_____

_____

_____

_____

_____

_____

What was your best subject in school, and what was your worst subject?

_____

_____

_____

Did you ever visit the principal's office?

_____

_____

_____

_____

Describe the meanest teacher you ever had in school or the class you least preferred to attend.

_____

_____

_____

_____

What kind of antics would go on when you had a substitute in the classroom? Describe an example.

_____

_____

_____

_____

Describe a trip to the library when you were a child. Did you have your own library card? What kinds of books did you like to read?

_____

_____

_____

_____

_____

_____

Describe a trip downtown or to the "big city" that you had as a youngster.

_____

_____

_____

_____

_____

_____

What was your greatest fear as a child? Why do you think you were so afraid of this?

_____

_____

_____

_____

How old were you when you learned how to ride a bike? Who taught you?

Who taught you to swim, and where did you learn?

What was an adventure you remember as a child?

Did you have a favorite movie?

Who were your childhood crushes?

Did you have your own room? If not, who did you share a room with?

What was your favorite room in your house growing up?

Did your family ever move? If so, how many times, and why? What was your reaction to moving?

Did you play sports growing up? What did you play?

Who was your favorite movie star, singer, or athlete?

What was a common saying or term you and your friends used when you were growing up?

Beliefs & Values

Do you belong to a particular church or religious or civic organization?

What is your earliest memory of attending church with your family? If you never attended a church, what is your earliest memory of someone you love teaching you an important value, principle, or belief?

Do you consider yourself to be a person of faith? Why or why not?

Describe a time you remember being untruthful. What were the circumstances, and how did you feel about the experience afterward?

_____

_____

_____

_____

_____

_____

_____

_____

If you are religious, describe what you remember about attending church as a child.

_____

_____

_____

_____

_____

_____

Describe an average Saturday or Sunday from your childhood.

_____

Have you ever had a difficult time forgiving someone for something? What happened?

What are your thoughts about prayer? Have you ever had a prayer answered in a miraculous way?

Describe any work you have ever done to provide
humanitarian service to someone less fortunate than you.

Describe a time when you experienced a terrible loss. How did you begin to heal from or overcome the loss?

Have you ever done something dishonest you regretted? How did you make amends? What advice would you give your children or grandchildren to help them avoid making the same mistake?

_____

_____

_____

_____

_____

_____

_____

_____

_____

_____

Do you have a favorite Bible story or scripture story? What is it?

_____

_____

_____

_____

_____

Is there a family story that was told over and over again that taught you a particular value? (Why it's important to tell the truth, why you should never give up, why you should never criticize another person, and so on.)

_____

_____

_____

_____

_____

_____

_____

Did you serve in your church? What was your favorite way to serve?

_____

_____

_____

What do you firmly believe in?

_____

_____

_____

_____

What advice would you give your children about faith?

_____

_____

_____

_____

_____

_____

_____

_____

_____

_____

_____

What were some of your favorite religious or spiritual activities and traditions?

_____

_____

_____

_____

Did you have your own scriptures? If so, when were they given to you? By whom?

_____

_____

_____

What is one spiritual experience that changed the course of your life?

_____

_____

_____

_____

_____

_____

_____

_____

_____

_____

_____

_____

_____

_____

_____

If you could go back and understand one truth earlier, what would that be?

_____

_____

_____

_____

_____

_____

_____

_____

When was the first time you remember feeling the Spirit?

_____

_____

_____

_____

_____

_____

_____

_____

What prayer was not answered how you wanted it to be, but it turned out for the best?

_____

_____

_____

_____

_____

_____

_____

_____

_____

_____

_____

_____

_____

_____

_____

_____

_____

_____

_____

_____

_____

_____

_____

_____

Activity

The Most Important Thing about Grandma

Thoughts and Memories
from Your Grandchildren

This section is reserved for your grandchildren to write in. Give each of them an opportunity to write their thoughts about the most important thing they have learned from you. Alternately, they may prefer to write their best memory of you. We've left blank pages for grandchildren who prefer to draw their happiest memories. Don't forget to have your grandchildren date and sign the page.

_____

_____

_____

_____

_____

_____

_____

_____

_____

_____

_____

_____

_____

Careers & Jobs

What was your first job, and what wage did you earn? Describe the working conditions and anything unusual about your job.

_____

_____

_____

_____

_____

_____

_____

_____

What did you do with the cash you earned from your earliest jobs?

_____

_____

_____

What is something you bought or paid for with your own money that you were excited about?

_____

_____

_____

_____

Describe any chores you were expected to do around your home growing up.

_____

_____

_____

_____

_____

How was housework or yardwork different than now?

_____

_____

_____

_____

What labor-saving device or appliance most transformed your daily work routine when it was invented?

_____

_____

_____

_____

_____

_____

_____

What was the most unique job you've ever had?

Did you ever start any kind of entrepreneurial adventure?

Did you or anyone in your family serve in the military? If so, what do you want your grandchildren to know about the experience?

Describe a typical day at work in your chosen career. What duties did you enjoy the most?

Describe your most annoying coworker, and tell what made him or her so difficult to work with.

_____

_____

_____

_____

_____

Was there a boss or supervisor who taught you something significant or important you used for the rest of your career?

_____

_____

_____

_____

_____

How do you feel your career allowed you to make a difference in the world?

_____

_____

_____

_____

_____

_____

Did you ever go on a memorable business trip or attend a conference that impacted your career in a significant way? Describe it.

Would you recommend your career to your grandchildren? Why or why not?

If you had your whole life to do over again, is there another career you think you would like to pursue?

Were there any barriers to employment you had to overcome?

What is the most significant contribution you ever made to your employer in terms of an idea, process, or habit that helped make the company more profitable or successful?

Were you ever fired from a job? Can you tell about the experience and what you learned from it?

_____

_____

_____

_____

_____

_____

What job did you love the most?

_____

_____

_____

_____

_____

_____

_____

_____

What job did you have that you worked the hardest at and made the least amount of money?

How did you choose your occupation?

When did you decide you had landed your dream job?

If you could have your grandchildren experience one of the jobs or chores you used to do consistently that they never have to do, what would it be? What would you hope for them to learn from it?

_____

_____

_____

_____

_____

_____

_____

_____

_____

_____

What career accomplishment are you most proud of?

_____

_____

_____

_____

_____

_____

Did your parents want you to choose the profession you did?

What time did you go to and get home from work each day?

Activity
Comfort Food

Many grandmothers are known for what they produce in the kitchen. Whether you know how to bake the perfect dinner roll or you have always been the "let's go out for dinner" kind of grandma, your grandchildren will have memories of the meals you prepared for them or times you spent together with food as the focal point.

Use the following pages to document anything you think your grandchildren will want to remember about your expertise (or lack thereof) in the kitchen.

Record the recipe for the one thing your children or grandchildren always ask you to fix when they visit you.

_____

_____

_____

_____

_____

_____

_____

_____

_____

Describe or record the recipe for **your own favorite** comfort food. What is the one dish you turn to that makes bad days better?

_____

_____

_____

_____

_____

_____

_____

Do you have an **heirloom recipe** in your kitchen—something passed on to you by your own mother or grandmother?

_____

_____

_____

_____

_____

_____

_____

Write down a recipe for your favorite **nonfood concoction**. This could be your recipe for playdough or papier-mâché paste. It could be the recipe for the smelly solution you use to drive away the deer that keep eating your tulips, the paste your grandmother applied to bee stings, or the homemade formula you use for polishing your silver. If there's a home remedy you know works, make sure you preserve it here for posterity!

Love

Where did you go on your first date, and who was with you?

What was the most unusual or creative date you ever went on?

Did you ever ask someone on a date or answer an invitation to a date in a unique way?

Describe the outfit your spouse was wearing the first time you met or any other details you remember about the first time you saw your spouse.

Describe your first date with your spouse. What was it about him that attracted you to him?

Describe two characteristics you most admire in your spouse.

_____

_____

_____

_____

_____

_____

_____

_____

_____

What do you remember about your first kiss? What about the first time you kissed your spouse?

_____

_____

_____

_____

_____

_____

_____

_____

Describe some details about how your romance progressed.
What are some fun experiences you had while courting?

When did you first know you were in love?

How did you or your husband propose? What is the one emotion from that day that stands out above all the others?

_____

_____

_____

_____

_____

_____

_____

_____

_____

_____

_____

_____

_____

_____

_____

_____

_____

Did you ever buy your husband an expensive piece of jewelry or other accessory?

_____

_____

_____

_____

Where were you married? What are some of the details that stand out about your wedding day? (If you have been married more than once, share details about each wedding.)

_____

_____

_____

_____

_____

_____

_____

_____

_____

_____

_____

_____

_____

_____

_____

_____

_____

_____

_____

Where did you go on your honeymoon? Are there any humorous or interesting stories you like to tell others about this time in your life?

_____

_____

_____

_____

_____

_____

_____

What is the most romantic thing your spouse ever did for you? Give details.

_____

_____

_____

_____

_____

_____

What would you consider to be the most romantic thing you've ever done for your spouse?

_____

_____

_____

_____

_____

_____

Did your husband call you by any pet names? Did those pet names change over the years?

_____

_____

_____

_____

_____

Do you treat your spouse better, worse, or about the same as you did while you were dating or courting?

_____

_____

_____

_____

What is the most important thing you have learned about being married?

What advice would you give your grandchildren about choosing a companion?

_____

_____

_____

_____

_____

_____

_____

_____

_____

What was your favorite date activity while you were dating?

_____

_____

_____

What is the worst date you ever went on?

_____

_____

_____

_____

What dance in high school was your most memorable?

_____

_____

_____

Did you ever feel guilty accepting a date? Why?

_____

_____

What qualities were you looking for in a spouse? Are those the same qualities that you would look for today?

_____

_____

_____

_____

_____

_____

_____

What kind of car did your spouse drive when
you met? Did he open the door for you?

_____

_____

_____

How long had you dated your spouse
before you met his family? What was
your first impression of them?

_____

_____

_____

_____

_____

Did you feel a spiritual connection with your spouse?

_____

_____

_____

_____

_____

_____

_____

How did you know your spouse was the right one?

When were you the angriest at your spouse?

Do you have a favorite love note from your spouse?
What did it say? If you have it, attach it here.

What did your parents think of your spouse?

Did you ever sneak out of the house to meet a date?

Influential People

What is the best advice anyone ever gave you? What was accomplished by following that advice?

_____

_____

_____

_____

_____

_____

_____

Who was your best friend in high school? Was there a time when you really leaned on and appreciated this friend?

_____

_____

_____

_____

_____

_____

_____

_____

Who is your "oldest" friend?

_____

_____

_____

Name two of your most influential high school teachers and what they taught you.

_____

_____

_____

_____

_____

If you attended college, what professor influenced you the most, and why?

_____

_____

_____

_____

_____

Is there a coworker, business partner, boss, or supervisor you feel you owe a debt of gratitude to? Why?

_____

_____

_____

_____

Is there someone you once disliked who you later developed a more respectful relationship with? What changed?

_____

_____

_____

_____

Who taught you about faith?

_____

_____

_____

What do you remember most about your father's influence?

_____

_____

_____

_____

_____

_____

Were you closer to one grandfather than another? Why?

_____

_____

_____

_____

_____

_____

_____

What do you remember most about your mother's influence?

_____

_____

_____

_____

_____

_____

_____

_____

_____

_____

_____

Who was your favorite example or role model growing up?

What is the quality you value most in a friend?

Which sibling would you want to be compared to?

Activity

In Her Own Words

Recording Your Voice

One of the treasured memories you can preserve for your family, using a host of new technologies, is a simple audio or video recording. With mobile device technology, there's almost no excuse not to have recordings of several special moments.

> *"One of the treasured memories you can preserve for your family, using a host of new technologies, is a simple audio or video recording."*

One of the largest family history–related sites on the Internet is FamilySearch.org. FamilySearch has created a "Memories" app that allows users to quickly record photos and voice memos and upload these "memories" to the FamilySearch website. Stories archived on the site will be accessible for generations to come. The fun thing about this resource is that it will allow you to record multiple stories about your life in your own voice. Visit the app website for details: FamilySearch.org/mobile/memories. With the app, you simply record yourself telling a story from your personal history using a smartphone or mobile device. Once the recording is completed and saved, you can instantly upload the recording to the FamilySearch website. (You can also tag the names of other family members mentioned in the story.) Once you attach a story to a specific individual's FamilySearch profile, people outside of your immediate family will not be able to see or access these recordings until after the individual is deceased. This helps maintain privacy for living persons.

Note to grandchildren: Take the time to sit Grandma down and record at least three or four of her favorite personal stories. Generations of future grandchildren and great-grandchildren will thank you someday. It will give them the ability to hear her voice and learn about her personality in ways that written documents can't capture.

Use some of the questions from this book as inspiration, set your mobile device on a stable surface, and capture Grandma's legacy. Then create a permanent record for others to enjoy. She'll probably be uneasy the first time you try it. People are often uncomfortable hearing their own recorded voice or watching a video of themselves, so you may need to try a couple of times to get your grandma to warm up to the idea.

If you decide to upload your recordings to FamilySearch, keep these important points in mind:

1. Make sure you add a detailed title to your recording so others will know what it is about and will be enticed to listen.

2. Remember that it's usually best to record short two-to-three-minute segments and upload several of them than it is to upload a single long recording that includes several stories.

Education

Describe your most memorable first day of school after you left elementary school.

_____

_____

_____

_____

_____

_____

Describe your most memorable day in junior high or high school.

_____

_____

_____

_____

Think of a time when a teacher said or did something that hurt your feelings. Write it down.

_____

_____

_____

_____

Do you have a memorized poem or section of prose you like to recite during difficult or important times in your life?

_____

_____

_____

_____

_____

_____

Did your education ever get cut short, and if so, why?

_____

_____

_____

_____

_____

What dream or goal did you have as a teenager that you accomplished? What about one you didn't accomplish?

_____

_____

_____

_____

_____

Think of a time when you got into the most trouble with a teacher. What did he or she do to handle the problem?

What was your high school mascot? What were your school colors? Did these influence the way you dressed at school, and if so, how?

Describe a typical high school date. Where did kids your age like to hang out, and what did you like to do on dates?

_____

_____

_____

_____

_____

_____

Did you ever attend a prom or formal dance? Describe the experience.

_____

_____

_____

_____

_____

_____

Describe any clubs or student organizations you joined.

_____

_____

_____

Can you remember a tragedy or other significant world event that happened when you were in high school? Did this affect your personal future at all?

_____

_____

_____

_____

_____

_____

_____

_____

_____

What award or accomplishment from your high school days stands out as the most significant?

_____

_____

_____

How many students were in your high school graduating class?

What did you do for your graduation celebration?

After high school, what was the next step in your life plan—work, college, vocational school, military, or humanitarian experience? Give some details about why you made that decision and why you are glad you took that path.

If you attended college or a vocational school, tell about what you studied and what you majored or minored in. If you completed a master's or doctorate degree, describe your thesis and dissertation.

Speaking to your grandchildren, what is the most important thing they can do after they graduate from high school to help prepare them for life?

_____

_____

_____

_____

_____

_____

_____

_____

_____

Tell about any roommates you had, including quirky habits they had and the kinds of things you would do for fun when you weren't working or studying.

_____

_____

_____

_____

_____

_____

During your early twenties, what kind of recreational pursuits did you enjoy as a break from the routine, work, and school?

Did you like to learn?

What was the one thing you wish you would have paid more attention to in school?

Did you drive a car to school? What kind?

What was your favorite subject?

Were you ever teased or bullied?

_____

_____

_____

_____

_____

Did you receive a scholarship or grant?

_____

_____

_____

_____

Did you ever feel like giving up? Name one experience when you weren't sure school was for you.

_____

_____

_____

_____

_____

_____

_____

Did your parents encourage education? Did they expect you to attend college?

_____

_____

_____

_____

_____

Was there a class or teacher that helped you decide what career path to take? How did the class or teacher spark your interest?

_____

_____

_____

_____

_____

_____

_____

_____

Hobbies & Pastimes

What sports did you play as a child?

_____

_____

_____

_____

Did you ever have your photo in a newspaper?

_____

_____

_____

_____

Have you ever entered a project or an item into a fair, contest, or competition? Why did you win or lose?

_____

_____

_____

_____

_____

_____

As a child, did you take any kind of lessons? If so, describe the teacher and what you learned.

_____

_____

_____

_____

Did you ever have an experience with losing a contest or hearing someone criticize something you were really proud of? What was your reaction?

_____

_____

_____

_____

_____

What is one talent you started to develop but gave up? Why did you stop?

_____

_____

_____

_____

What is one talent you think you could have really excelled in if time, desire, or money had been more plentiful?

_____

_____

_____

_____

Have you ever performed in public? If so, what was your most memorable performance?

Have you ever participated on a team? Think of two or three examples and tell what was memorable about it.

Describe a teammate you admired or despised and why you felt the way you did.

What act of selfless service did you perform at one time in your life that required more of you than you expected it to? Describe what happened.

_____

_____

_____

_____

_____

_____

_____

_____

Was there ever a pet in your home you had a special relationship with?

_____

_____

_____

_____

Do you have any memorable experiences hunting, fishing, or working with animals in the wild?

_____

_____

_____

Recall a visit to a theme park or fair that did or didn't turn out like you expected.

_____

_____

_____

_____

_____

_____

_____

_____

_____

_____

Describe the worst campout you ever went on.

_____

_____

_____

_____

Concert, rodeo, or baseball game—which would you choose, and why?

_____

_____

_____

Did you ever take swimming lessons?

_____

_____

Describe one of your hobbies and how you developed an interest in that hobby.

_____

_____

_____

If time and money were unlimited, what hobby would you have taken up when you were in your prime, and why? What hobby would you start now?

_____

_____

What was your favorite Saturday pastime?

What age were you when you first saw the ocean?

If you could choose, in hindsight, one thing you wish you had participated in during high school, what would it be?

Who was your favorite coach?

Activity

Instagramming Grandma

Here's a fun activity that any grandchild with a mobile device can help you complete. Have your grandchild document you with ten photos of their choosing and post one favorite to Instagram using the hashtag #InstagrammingGrandma. There you'll find fun photos that other *Grandma's Storybook* readers have taken with their grandmothers, and you may just find some inspiration.

Start with some of these ideas for your grandkids:

☐ Grandma in her kitchen

☐ Grandma in her garden or yard, in front of her house, or in a location you would commonly find her (for example, in a favorite chair)

☐ her with something that is related to one of her hobbies (a sewing machine, a computer, a scrapbook, a piano, and so on)

☐ her oldest, most vintage kitchen gadget

☐ her favorite room

- [ ] her nightstand (make sure your photo shows everything on her nightstand)

- [ ] her hands

- [ ] Grandma holding her most priceless possession

- [ ] her game closet, toy chest, playroom, or the place you liked to spend time when you were a child

- [ ] your favorite toy to play with at Grandma's house

- [ ] your favorite hiding place at Grandma's house

- [ ] Grandma with something she made or built

- [ ] a truly candid photo of Grandma with Grandpa

As an alternative, sit down with your grandchild and tell him or her you are going to create a time capsule of the twenty most important photos of you that exist. What photos would your grandchild choose? What photos would you choose if you were choosing your favorites?

Consider the following:

- How will the family preserve these important photos?

- Who will be responsible to keep and care for the originals?

- How can copies of the originals be made available to anyone who is interested? (See page 99 for information about using the FamilySearch "Memories" app to preserve a copy online for extended family and future generations to access.)

- Are there other photos in your collection that include pictures of people only you can identify?

- What is the best way to document and archive your most precious family photos?

Places You Have Lived

What was the community of your childhood like? What did your neighborhood look like?

_____

_____

_____

_____

_____

_____

_____

Can you remember any details about the home you grew up in (or your favorite place to live if you moved around a lot)?

_____

_____

_____

_____

_____

_____

Describe your first apartment or home when you moved away from your parents' home for the first time.

_____

_____

Would you prefer to live in the city or the country if you were twenty-one again and just starting out? Why?

Think of a neighbor who had an impact on you. Was he or she friendly or grouchy? Why does the memory of that person stand out to you?

What did you do with the other friends who lived in your neighborhood during the summer?

_____

_____

_____

_____

_____

_____

_____

_____

Have you ever had a get-together or block party with your neighbors?

_____

_____

_____

Describe your neighborhood as an adult. What neighbors do you remember best, and why?

_____

_____

_____

_____

How many times did you move growing up?

_____

_____

_____

_____

_____

_____

If you could choose any place to live now, where would that be?

_____

_____

_____

_____

_____

_____

Did you ever hate living somewhere? What about it did you hate?

_____

_____

_____

_____

_____

_____

_____

_____

_____

What's the longest you ever lived somewhere?

_____

_____

_____

_____

_____

_____

_____

_____

How close were you to your church or place of worship?

_____

_____

_____

_____

_____

Health & Medical

Did you ever have a childhood disease that children are now vaccinated against? Mumps? Polio? Measles? Chicken pox? Describe what it was like.

_____

_____

_____

_____

_____

_____

What was the strangest medicine you ever had to take as a child? Why did you need to take it?

_____

_____

_____

_____

_____

Describe what it was like to be sick as a child.

_____

_____

_____

_____

Were there any home remedies used in your family to cure illness or injury? Can you describe in detail how this worked?

_____

_____

_____

_____

_____

What is the worst injury you have ever sustained? Describe the experience.

_____

_____

_____

_____

_____

Have you ever broken a bone? How did it happen?

_____

_____

_____

_____

Were there any unique medical events related to the births of any of your children?

Talk about your most memorable trip to the dentist or what you remember a visit to the dentist being like when you were young.

Did you ever see an orthodontist? What strange and unique orthodontic devices did you wear as a child or as an adult?

_____

_____

_____

_____

Were you afraid of the dentist?

_____

_____

_____

Did you ever have a faith-building experience that had to do with your health?

_____

_____

_____

_____

If you could change one part of your medical history, what would it be?

_____

_____

Did you have a hard time conceiving children?

If you could have had one medical miracle, what would that be?

Were you ever in a car accident?

Ancestry & Heritage

What's your mother's name and birthplace?

What's your father's name and birthplace?

If your mother or father has passed away, what do you recall about their death? How old were you at the time?

What do you want your children to know about your mother?

_____

_____

_____

_____

_____

_____

What characteristic do you most admire about your mother?

_____

_____

_____

_____

_____

_____

What was your favorite thing to do with your mother?

_____

_____

_____

_____

_____

What do you want your children to know about your father?

_____
_____
_____
_____
_____
_____
_____

What characteristic do you most admire about your father?

_____
_____
_____
_____
_____
_____
_____

What was your favorite thing to do with your father?

_____
_____
_____
_____
_____
_____

What is the one story your mother told over and over about herself?

_____

_____

_____

_____

_____

What was your parents' most common form of discipline when you were disobedient? Do you agree or disagree with their methods?

_____

_____

_____

_____

What hobby or talent was your dad known for?

_____

_____

_____

What hobby or talent was your mom known for?

_____

_____

_____

What is one story you heard your father tell about himself more than once?

_____

_____

_____

_____

_____

_____

What is a phrase you heard your mother say often?

_____

_____

What is a phrase you heard your father say often?

_____

_____

_____

_____

Write down something you remember about watching your dad get ready for work.

_____

_____

_____

What smell reminds you of your mom? Why?

_____

_____

_____

_____

What parenting advice did your parents or others give you that you implemented in your own home with some success?

_____

_____

_____

_____

_____

Who was your favorite aunt or uncle? Why?

_____

_____

_____

What was your favorite thing to do with your grandpa?

_____

_____

_____

_____

Did you live near any extended family growing up?

_____

_____

_____

_____

What phrase did you hate hearing your mom say?

_____

_____

_____

How did you know when your dad was proud of you?

_____

_____

_____

Did you ever have an experience where you felt really close to your mother?

_____

_____

_____

_____

_____

_____

_____

_____

What car did your grandparents drive?

_____

_____

What do you wish your father would have told you?

_____

_____

_____

_____

_____

What's the best advice your grandma gave you?

Activity

Live Your Funeral Today

Begin Today with the End in Mind

This exercise isn't intended to be sad or morbid. Instead, it's an opportunity for you to really think about how you want your children, grandchildren, and friends to celebrate your life. Imagine that you have lived to a ripe old age. You have had time to accomplish all that you wanted to, and now you have passed away and it's time for your friends and family to hold a memorial service to celebrate your life. What do you hope people will say about you?

What are three personality traits you have that you hope speakers at your memorial service would comment on as your defining characteristics?

1.

2.

3.

When your grandchildren recall a happy event from your lifetime, what day do you hope will stand out in their memories?

What will they observe about your community
service or your devotion to your fellow man?

_____

_____

_____

_____

_____

Who would you most like to have
speak at your memorial service?

_____

_____

_____

_____

_____

_____

What are one or two significant accomplishments you've
had so far in your life that you hope will be mentioned in
your obituary?

_____

_____

_____

_____

_____

What story or humorous event do you think your grandchildren or children might use to illustrate the kind of relationship you had with your spouse?

_____

_____

_____

_____

_____

_____

What imperfection do you know they will love you for, even
though you worked your whole life to overcome it?

_____

_____

_____

_____

_____

What meaningful activity did you pursue for as long as
your body would let you continue?

_____

_____

_____

_____

_____

_____

Rank the following list of things your family could say about you in order of importance (1 is the most important to you, and 8 is the least important). If something from this list seems unimportant to you, cross it off and write in your own.

___ The world is a better place because she was in it. She knew how to make everyone feel important.

___ She knew what was important in life. Her _____ came before everything else.

___ She was faithful to her religion, her spouse, and her own sense of morals.

___ Her family is going to miss her, but she taught them everything they need to know to thrive.

___ She left her worldly affairs in order. She managed her resources well and knew how to be thrifty, and her finances were never a burden to her family.

___ She lived life to the fullest. She was full of vigor, happiness, and a zest for life. It was a joy to be around her.

___ She never wasted anything.

___ She was constantly learning. She never stopped acquiring new knowledge.

Travel, Technology & Historic Moments

What is your dream car?

Describe your first car. What did you like about it? How much did it cost? What was unique about it?

Think of three unusual forms of transportation you have used. What were the circumstances?

Did you ever get a flat tire or have car problems when it was particularly inconvenient?

Describe a time when you were stranded. What happened? How did you get yourself out of the situation?

When was the first time you remember using a computer?

What was your experience like the first time you sent an email?

Describe your first computer. What were you amazed that it could do?

Describe your first cell phone and everything you used it for. What did it look like? What was something amazing that you could do with it that no one would be impressed with now? What was the most frustrating thing about it?

Name something that has been invented in your lifetime that you now use every day, other than a computer or cell phone.

When you hear the word *drive-in*, what picture comes to your mind? Describe it.

Describe a time you were pulled over for a traffic violation.

Tell about a time when you traveled to a foreign country.
If you have never traveled, where would you go, given the
chance?

_____

_____

_____

_____

_____

_____

_____

_____

_____

_____

_____

_____

_____

_____

What is the largest meeting (not a sporting event) you
ever attended? Where was the meeting, and what was the
purpose?

_____

_____

_____

What would you consider to be the most significant world event that has taken place in your lifetime?

_____

_____

_____

_____

_____

Tell about how you learned to ride a bike.

_____

_____

_____

Who taught you how to drive? Describe your earliest memories of what it was like to be behind the wheel, including what you drove and any accidents you had.

_____

_____

_____

_____

_____

_____

_____

What cartoon or TV program did you love as a child?

_____

_____

Describe the first video game you ever played. What was your favorite video or computer game, and why?

_____

_____

Describe the first day a man landed on the moon. Where were you, and what do you remember about the day?

_____

_____

_____

Describe the first time you remember watching a color TV.

_____

_____

_____

What was the first movie you remember watching? Describe the theater, the movie, and anything else that is different from watching movies now.

_____

_____

_____

_____

Describe what you remember about any of the following:

The fall of the twin towers on 9/11

The fall of the Berlin Wall

A presidential assassination or assassination of a key figure

The *Challenger* disaster

A war that started during your lifetime

Activity

Pinteresting Facts about Grandma

Crowdsourcing Happy Memories

Ask your children and grandchildren to gather as many photos from the Internet as possible to document your life. Actual photos are fine, but the real point of this exercise is to have your children document what reminds them of you. One fun way to do this is to create a shared Pinterest board or have someone in your family create one for you. (Pinterest is a web and app-based platform that allows you to gather and "pin" photos, project ideas, and more.) Visit AGenerousThought.com/pinteresting-history to view an example.

Once an item has been "pinned," the author can add a comment about why this object reminds them of you: "Mom used pink foam rollers like these in my hair every night and then brushed out my curls every morning. I hated the snarls!" or "We had a calico cat named Freckles that loved to sit at Mom's feet while she folded the socks," or "Grandma never missed an episode of *Days of Our Lives*!"

Your children will be able to describe much of your life in ways that will surprise you. The images they pull up out of the recesses of their own memories will give everyone a truly unique perspective on some of the intangibles of their relationship with you and what memories they have stored away to tell their own children about.

Here are some ideas to get your children and grandchildren thinking about what they can pin to your shared Pinterest board:

- photos that represents something about her favorite hobby

- images of the location where she went to school (check for images online)

- photos of any items that remind you specifically of her (the brand of breath mints she keeps in her purse, her favorite book, the style of work boots she wore on the farm, the pattern for her china dishes, and so on)

- images of any instruments she plays, favorite groups or styles of music she likes to listen to, the album cover for her favorite album, and so on

- a link to the trailer for her all-time favorite movie

- photos of any exotic (or not-so-exotic) places where you traveled with her (camping trips, cruises, flights, theme parks, and so on)

- quirky things about her personality, like how she always wore an oversized pair of paint-splattered overalls in her artist's studio or that she is still backpacking at age sixty-five

- images of her favorite beverage

- two or three things you expect to find in her pantry or snacks that she would typically serve to visitors

- fragrances that remind you of her (What is her favorite brand of soap, lotion, or perfume? Does her house smell like cats, cut flowers, or baking bread?)

- photos of her at several stages of life: childhood, a high school yearbook photo, at her wedding, and the most recent photo you can find

- common items in her home you would find at a flea market or in an antique shop fifty years from now that would evoke fond memories (Think "vintage" and "antiques road show.")

Completely
Random Questions

What is the biggest hole you have ever dug, and why did you dig it?

Did you ever have a brush with the law? Describe it.

Were you ever lost in a remote place?

Do you have a favorite meal? Is it different or the same as when you were a child?

Think of a time when you were most afraid. Why? What happened?

Was there a storm you experienced that was unusual or memorable? What happened? Were you prepared, afraid, or in awe?

Think of two or three songs that are your favorites. Why are they important to you, and who are the artists?

If it were a "blue sky" day and you had no other obligations, what would you do with your time? Write down the details of another "blue sky" day that stands out as a memorable or happy day.

When was a time you were totally alone?

What is the closest you have ever come to experiencing a natural disaster? If you survived one or more disasters, share the details and how experiencing that event affected you personally.

_____

_____

_____

_____

_____

_____

_____

_____

_____

_____

What was a fashion trend you got really excited about?

_____

_____

Describe a birthday party you had as an adult. What stood out about it? Who was present, and how did you celebrate?

_____

_____

_____

_____

_____

What is a compliment someone gave you once that you
still remember? Who gave you the compliment, and why was
it so meaningful? _____

_____

_____

_____

_____

_____

What is your favorite dessert? Describe a time when you
recall eating this dessert. _____

_____

_____

What music, hymn, or song would you like to have performed
at your funeral? Why? _____

_____

_____

Have you ever witnessed something you consider to be a miracle?

_____

_____

_____

_____

_____

_____

_____

_____

_____

What is the dirtiest you have ever been?

_____

_____

_____

_____

_____

What is the hungriest you have ever been?

_____

_____

_____

_____

_____

Has your life ever been in danger? Describe the circumstances and how you were protected.

_____

_____

_____

_____

_____

Have you ever had to hide from someone or something? Describe the experience.

_____

_____

_____

_____

_____

What was the most embarrassing thing that ever happened to you?

_____

_____

_____

_____

_____

Activity

Googling Grandma
& Documenting the Documents

While you are seated at a computer together, have one of your grandchildren show you what they can learn about you using only your name as an Internet search term. It may surprise you both what you will discover. Have your grandchild type your name into an Internet browser (put quotation marks around your name for a more exact search), and you may be shocked how many or how few facts the two of you can document. Try different versions of your name (search by your maiden name or include your initials) to get different results. Keep in mind that if you don't leave other records with your family members, this is all your great-grandchildren will know about you. Is the record complete enough to satisfy you or them?

Your life history can be sparsely pieced together just from a few simple documents. Consider how much you would know about a person if all you had access to was an obituary. Family history gurus get excited about details as simple as a birthdate or the name of a spouse, because having one piece of accurate information often makes it possible to trace other pieces. You can make the family genealogist's job much easier by compiling originals or copies of a few simple documents. It's easy to store these in a large three-ring binder, using acid-free plastic sheet protectors. The list of documents below pertains specifically to items that will tell part of your story, but as long as you are collecting documents to keep together in one safe place, consider adding important papers such as insurance policies or a copy of your will or trust. Speak with a financial planner for a complete list of documents your heirs will need in order to settle your estate.

- [ ] your birth certificate
- [ ] your marriage certificate
- [ ] your written journals or day planner records
- [ ] photo albums, scrapbooks, or a typewritten page documenting their existence and location
- [ ] any important letters or correspondence you have saved
- [ ] your passport or other travel documents
- [ ] your diploma or degree certificates
- [ ] your military records and awards
- [ ] a copy of your business card or stationery
- [ ] school awards, trophies, or certificates
- [ ] medical and health records

Thoughts

If you've written even a single page in this book, congratulations! You've just turned your edition of *Grandma's Storybook* into a family heirloom. You've also created a record of your own life in your own words and by your own hand so that your children's children's children will be able to access their own family narrative. That connection to you will be an important part of what they need to get them through rough days and give them a renewed appreciation for their own opportunities and blessings. Looking into the palms of their own hands, they will see you there. They will know you and love you. Even better, they will know you love them.

That Reminds Me

Often, as you begin writing your story, you'll recall a special event, story, or thought you know should be recorded, and you won't want to leave those stories out! Use these final pages to jot down any stories you don't want to "slip through the cracks" and be forgotten.